WHAT DOES GOD EXPECT AND REQUIRE OF CHRISTIANS?

WHAT DOES
GOD EXPECT
AND REQUIRE OF
CHRISTIANS?

ACCORDING TO
NEW TESTAMENT
SCRIPTURES

JESSIE CLARK
XULON PRESS

Xulon Press
2301 Lucien Way #415
Maitland, FL 32751
407.339.4217
www.xulonpress.com

Unless otherwise indicated, Scripture quotations taken from the King James Version (KJV) – *public domain.*

Paperback ISBN-13: 978-1-6628-5241-1
Ebook ISBN-13: 978-1-6628-5242-8

Table of Contents

Introduction

If you are a Christian, whether you are new or have been one for a long time, you need to know and understand what God (not man or the church) expects and requires of you.

Many Christians have a false sense of understanding of what Christianity is all about because of teachings, what they have been exposed to, and what they have seen passed down from generation to generation.

This book is written in a way to help you more easily know and understand what our heavenly Father expects and requires of you.

The scriptures let us know that those things written of old were written for our learning (Romans 15:4). And, that all scriptures are given by the inspiration of God and is profitable for doctrine, for reprimand, for correction, for instruction in righteousness (II Timothy 3:16, 17). However, this book will focus on the teachings of Jesus and his apostles/disciples found within the New Testament scriptures.

Purpose of this book

Please know that there is a lot of information covered in this book. It would be so easy for you to just read over the words and not benefit from why this book was written.

You must keep in mind that you are a child of God and just like with parents there are expectations and requirements for a child to follow.

My hope is that you internalize this information and that you are encouraged and inspired to live (or continue to live) a life that is pleasing to your heavenly Father.

After reading this book, it is my prayer that you will know and under-stand what kind of relationship you should have with your heavenly Father and with your brothers and sisters in Christ; the person you are to be; the life you are to live; and what is expected and required of the church body. This book will also inform you of harmful influences that can affect your spiritual wellbeing. As well as, what you need to do to be ready when Jesus returns.

What Does God Expect and Require of Christians?

According to New Testament Scriptures

In Our Relationship with God

What Does God Expect and Require of Christians?
In Our Relationship with God

Know Him

- We know that the Son of God is come, and hath given us an understanding, **that we may know him** that is true. *Ref. I John 5:20*

- Without faith it is impossible to please him: for he that cometh to God **must believe that he is**. *Ref. Hebrews. 11:6*

- (His) sheep **follow him**, for they **know his voice**. *Ref. John 10:4*

- **If** you continue in (Jesus) word, *then* are you (his) disciples; indeed, and **you will know the truth**, and the truth shall make you free. *Ref. John 8:31, 32*

- **Draw nigh (come closer) to God**, and **He will draw nigh to you**. *Ref. James 4:8*

- **God is love;** he that dwell in love **dwell in God**, and God in him. *Ref. I John 4:16-18*

- Jesus is the good shepherd, and know (his) *sheep*, and **(his sheep knows him)**. (His) sheep hear (his) voice, and (Jesus) know them, and they follow (Jesus): And (Jesus) give unto them eternal life; and they shall never perish, neither shall any *man* pluck them out of (Jesus) hand. *Ref. John 10:14, 27, 28*

- He that **has** (Jesus) **commandments**, and **keep them**, he it is that **love (Jesus)**: and he that love (Jesus) shall be loved of (his) Father, and (Jesus) will love him, and **will manifest (himself) to him.** *Ref. John 14:21*

- **We know him, if we keep his commandments.** *Ref. I John 2:3*

Trust Him

- **Faith,** if it hath not works **(without actions)**, is dead, being alone. *Ref. James 2:17*

- Now **faith** is the **substance of things hoped for**, the **evidence of things not seen.** *Ref. Hebrews 11:1*

- Without **faith** it is impossible to please him: for **he that cometh to God** must **believe** that he is, and **that he is a rewarder of them that diligently seek him**. *Ref. Hebrews 11:6*

- Whosoever shall say unto this mountain, be thou removed, and be thou cast into the sea; and shall **not doubt in his heart** but shall **believe** that those things which he saith shall come to pass; he shall have whatsoever he saith...what things soever ye desire, **when ye pray, believe that ye receive *them*, and ye shall have *them*.** *Ref. Mark 11:23, 24*

- **Ask**, and it shall be given you; **seek**, and ye shall find; **knock**, and it shall be opened unto you: for every one that (ask) (receive); and he that (seek) (find); and to him that (knock) it shall be opened... if ye then, being evil, know how to give good gifts unto your children, how much more shall your Father which is in heaven give **good things to them that ask him?** *Ref. Matthew 7:7, 8, 11*

- **Take no thought for your life,** what you shall eat; neither for the body, what ye shall put on... for all these things do the nations of the world seek after: and your Father (know) that you have need of these things. But rather **seek ye the kingdom of God**; and **all these things shall be added unto you**...for it is your Father's good pleasure to give you the kingdom. *Ref. Luke 12:22, 30-32*

- **Believe on (Jesus),** the works that (he did) you will do also; and **greater *works* than these shall he do;** because (Jesus) went unto (his) Father. *Ref. John 14:12*

- **If ye abide in me (Jesus),** and **(his) words abide in you, ye shall ask what ye will**, and it shall be done unto you. *Ref. John 15:7*

Depend on him

- **Come boldly** unto the throne of grace that we may obtain mercy and find grace to **help in time of need.** *Ref. Hebrews 4:16*

- The **Spirit** also **helps** our infirmities **(weaknesses): for we know not what we should pray for as we ought:** but the Spirit itself (make) intercession **(mediates)** for us with groanings which cannot be uttered. *Ref. Romans 8:26*

- **(Comforts) us in all our tribulation,** that we may be able to comfort them which are in any trouble, by the comfort wherewith we ourselves are comforted of God. *Ref. II Corinthians 1:4*

- Ye are the temple of the living God; as God hath said, **I will dwell in them,** and **walk in *them*;** and **I will be their God**, and they shall be my people...and **will be a Father unto you**, and **ye shall be my sons and daughters,** saith the Lord Almighty. *Ref. II Corinthians 6:16, 18*

- **Come unto (Jesus)**, all *ye* that labor and are heavy laden, and **(Jesus) will give you rest**. Take (his) yoke upon you and learn of (him); for (he) is meek and lowly in heart: and **you shall find rest unto your souls**. For (his) yoke *is* easy, and (his) burden is light. *Ref. Matthew 11:28-30*

- Jesus said unto them, (he's) the bread of life: **he that (come) to (him) shall never hunger**; and **he that (believe) on (him) shall never thirst**...him that (come) to (him) (he) will in no wise cast out. *Ref. John 6:35, 37*

- (Jesus) is the door: by (him) if any man enters in, he shall be saved, and shall go in and out, and find pasture **(comfort)**. (Jesus came) that they might have **life**, and **that they might have it more abundantly**. *Ref. John 10:9, 10*

- **Take no thought for your life** (what you will eat, drink and clothing)...your heavenly Father **knows what you need. Seek first** the **Kingdom of God**, and **his righteousness** and all these things will be added unto you. *Ref. Matt.6:25,32, 33*

What Does God Expect and Require of Christians?

According to New Testament Scriptures

In Our Relationship with Each Other

What Does God Expect and Require of Christians?
In Our Relationship with Each Other

Love...

- **one another**. *Ref. I John 3:11*

- **(laying) down our life** for the brethren. *Ref. I John 3:16*

- **not in words**...but in deed and in truth. *Ref. I John 3:18*

- **one another with a pure heart**. *Ref. I Peter 1:22*

- **thy neighbor as thyself**. *Ref. Luke 10:27*

- **your enemies,** and do good, and lend, hoping for nothing again. *Ref. Luke 6:35*

- **(increasing)** and abound in **love** one toward another, and toward all men. *Ref. I Thess. 3:12*

- **(being) kindly affectionate** to one another with brotherly love. *Ref. Romans 12:10*

- **having compassion** for one another, **love as brothers**. *Ref. I Peter 3:8*

- **(having) fervent (intensely) charity (love)** among yourselves. *Ref. I Peter 4:8*

Pray...

- **for another**, that you may be healed. The effectual (unceasing) fervent (passionate) **prayer of a righteous man avail much**. *Ref. James 5:16*

- **for them that despitefully use you.** *Ref. Luke 6:28*

Peace

- **Follow peace** with all men. *Ref. Hebrews 12:14*

- **Follow** after the **things which make for peace**. *Ref. Romans 14:19*

- **Live peaceably** with all men. *Ref. Romans 12:18*

Forgive

- **(Forgive) one another.** *Ref. Colossians 3:13*

- Be kind to one another, tenderhearted, **forgiving one another**. *Ref. Ephesian 4:32*

- **Forbearing (forgiving) one another in love** – striving to keep unity of the spirit in the bond of peace. *Ref. Ephesian 4:2, 3*

- If thy brother trespass against you, rebuke him, if he repents, **forgive him**. *Ref. Luke 17:3*

- **(If thy brother)** trespass **(sin) against (you)** seven times a day and say seven times a day...saying I repent...**forgive him**. *Ref. Luke 17:4*

- When ye stand praying, **forgive**, if you have an ought (issue) with any. *Ref. Mark 11:25*

- **Forgive** and you shall **(will) be forgiven**. Luke 6:37

Give to those in need

- If a **brother or sister** be **naked**, and destitute **(deprived) of daily food**. *Ref. James 2:15, 16*

- **Whoso** (has) **this world's good,** and (see) **his brother (has) need.** *Ref. I John 3:17*

- **Distributing** to the **necessity of the saints**. *Ref. Romans 12:13*

- **Give** to **every man** that (ask) of (you). *Ref. Luke 6:30*

- **Give,** and it shall be given to you. *Ref. Luke 6:38*

- If thine **enemy hunger**, feed him; if he **thirst**, give him drink. *Ref. Romans 12:20*

Help one another

- **Bear** ye one another's **burdens**. *Ref. Galatians 6:2*

- If a man be **overtaken in a fault**, ye which are spiritual, **restore** such an one in the **spirit of meekness**. *Ref. Galatians 6:1*

- Remember them...which suffer adversity **(hardship)**. *Ref. Hebrews 13:3*

- Be ye all of one mind, having **compassion** for one another, love as brethren, be pitiful **(sorry)**, be courteous **(polite)**. *Ref. I Peter 3:8, 9*

- As **every man** hath **received the gift**, even so **minister** the same one **to another**. *Ref. I Peter 4:10*

- If any of you do **(error) from the truth**, and one convert him...he which convert the sinner from the error of his way shall save a soul from death. *Ref. James 5:19, 20*

- **We** then **that are strong ought to bear the** infirmities **(weaknesses)** of the **weak** and not to please ourselves. *Ref. Romans 15:1*

- **Warn them** that are unruly, **comfort** the feebleminded, **support** the weak, be **patient** toward all men. *Ref. I Thessalonians 5:14*

- None render evil for evil unto any man; but ever **follow that which is good**, both among yourselves, and to all men. *Ref. I Thessalonians 5:15*

- (God) (comfort) us in all our tribulation (trouble), **that we may be able to comfort them which are in any trouble.** *Ref. II Corinthians 1:4*

- **Be gentle** unto all *men*, **apt to teach**, **patient**, in **meekness instructing those that oppose themselves**. *Ref. II Timothy 2:24, 25*

Encourage and support one another

- **Exhort (encourage)** one another daily. *Ref. Hebrews 3:13*

- **Support the weak**. *Ref. I Thessalonians 5:14*

- **Comfort** the feebleminded **(weak-minded)**. *Ref. I Thessalonians 5:14*

- **Condescend (humble yourself)** to **men of low estate**. *Ref. Romans 12:16*

- Every one of us **please his neighbor for his good** to **edification**. *Ref. Rom. 15:2*

- **Rejoice** (be happy) with them that rejoice, and **weep** with them that weep. *Ref. Romans 12:15*

- **Teaching** and **admonishing** one another in psalms and hymns and spiritual songs, singing with grace in your hearts to the Lord. *Ref. Colossians 3:16*

- In lowliness of mind let each of **esteem other** better than them-selves. *Ref. Philippians 2:3*

- **Look** not every man on his own things, but every man also **on the things of others**. *Ref. Philippians 2:4*

- **Remember them that are in bonds**, as bound with them; and them which **suffer** adversity **(hardship)**. *Ref. Hebrews 13:3*

You should...

- whatever **ye would that men should do to you, do ye even so to them**. *Ref. Matthew 7:12*

- **tell him (your brother) his fault (against you)** between thee and him alone: if he shall hear thee, thou hast gained thy brother. *Ref. Matthew 18:15*

- **bless them** that persecute (mistreat) you. **Rejoice** with them that do rejoice, and **weep** with them that weep. *Ref. Romans 12:14, 15*

- recompense **(repay) to no man evil for evil. Provide things honest** in the sight of all men. *Ref. Romans 12:17*

- **Live peaceably** with all me. *Ref. Romans 12:17*

- **confess your faults** one to another. *Ref. James 5:16*

- **(submit) yourselves** to one another. *Ref. Ephesians 5:21*

- **use hospitality** one to another without grudging. *Ref. I Peter 4:9, 10*

You should be...

- **of the same mind** one toward another...not wise in your own conceits. *Ref. Romans 12:16*

- **patient** toward all men. *Ref. I Thessalonian 5:14*

- **subject to** one another, and **clothed with humility**: for God (resist) the proud, and giveth grace to the humble. *Ref. I Peter 5:5-7*

- **good to them which hate you**. *Ref. Luke 6:27*

- **good to all men**, especially unto them who are of the household of faith. *Ref. Galatians 6:10*

Should not ...

- **put a stumbling block** or an occasion to fall in his brother's way. *Ref. Romans 14:13*

- **have respect of persons** (favoring the haves over those that have not). *Ref. James 2:1-9*

- **(speak) evil** one of another. *Ref. James 4:11*

- defraud **(deceive) his brother** in *any* matter. *Ref. I Thessalonians 4:6*

- **render evil for evil** unto any man; but ever follow that which is good, both among yourselves, and to all men. *Ref. I Thessalonians 5:15*

- **(lie)** one to another, seeing that ye have put old off the man with his deeds. *Ref. Colossians 3:9*

- **(be) angry** with his brother without cause. *Ref. Matt. 5:22*

- **condemn.** *Ref. Luke 6:37*

- **judge** one another. *Ref. Luke 6:37*

- **be desirous of vain glory**, provoking one another, envying one another. *Ref. Galatians 5:26*

Elder Men, Young Men, Elder Women and Young Women

- **Rebuke not an Elder,** but intreat him as a **father.** *Ref. I Timothy 5:1*

- **Intreat...younger men** as **brethren.** *Ref. I Timothy 5:1*

- **Intreat...elder women** as **mothers.** *Ref. I Timothy 5:2*

- **Intreat...younger women** as **sisters.** *Ref. I Timothy 5:2*

Children

- **Obey** your parents in all things, for this is **well pleasing unto the Lord**. *Ref. Colossians 3:20*

- **Obey** your parents in the Lord: for this is right. *Ref. Ephesians 6:1*

- **Honor thy father and mother...that it may be well with thee,** and thou **mayest live long on the earth.** *Ref. Ephesians 6:2, 3*

fathers

- **Provoke not your children to anger**, lest they be discouraged. *Ref. Colossians 3:21*

- **Bring them (your children) up** in the nature and admonition of the Lord. *Ref. Ephesians 6:4*

Husbands

- **Love your wives**, and **be not bitter against them.** *Ref. Colossians 3:19*

- The head of every man is Christ; and the **head of the woman is the man**. *Ref. I Corinthians 11:3*

- **Dwell with them (wives)** according to **knowledge, giving (honor) unto the wife...**that your prayers won't be hindered. *Ref. I Peter 3:7*

- **Love your wives**, even as Christ also loved the church, and gave himself for it. *Ref. Ephesians 5:25*

- **Love your wives** as your own bodies. He that loveth his wife loveth himself. *Ref. Ephesians 5:28-30*

Wives

- **Submit yourselves** unto **your own husbands**, as unto the Lord. *Ref. Ephesians 5:22*

- **Be in subjection to your own husbands**. *Ref. I Peter 3:1*

- **Whose** adorning **(beautifying) let it not be** that **outward adorning (beautifying) of plaiting the hair, and wearing of gold, or putting on of apparel;** But let it be the hidden man of the heart...**a meek and quiet spirit**....which in the **sight of God a great price**. *Ref. I Peter 3:3, 4*

Marriage

- For this cause shall a man leave his father and mother, and shall be joined unto wife, and they **two shall be one flesh**. *Ref. Ephesians 5:31*

- Whosoever **put away his wife,** saving for the cause of fornication, causeth her to commit adultery: and whosoever shall marry her that is divorced committeth adultery. *Ref. Matthew 5:32*

- What therefore **God hath joined together**, let no put asunder. *Ref. Matthew 19:6*

- Let every (man/woman) have **(their own wife or husband)**. *Ref. I Corinthians 7:2*

- Let the (husband/wife) render **(give) due benevolence** – (husband/wife) hath not power of (his/her) own body. *Ref. I Corinthians 7:3, 4*

- Defraud **(deprive) ye not one the other**, except it be with consent for a time, that ye may give yourselves to fasting and prayer. *Ref. I Corinthians 7:5*

- **Let not the wife depart from her husband...if she depart**, let her remain unmarried, or be reconciled to her husband: and let not the husband put away his wife. *Ref. I Corinthians 7:10, 11*

Unmarried and Widows

- If any man or women that believeth have widows, let them relieve **(help) them**, and **let the church not be charged**. *Ref. I Timothy 5:16*

- He that is unmarried **careth for things** that belong to the Lord, **how he might please the Lord: But he that is married careth for the things that are of the world, how he may please his wife.** *Ref. I Corinthians 7:32, 33*

What Does God Expect and Require of Christians?

According to New Testament Scriptures

Be A Godly Person

What Does God Expect and Require of Christians?
Be A Godly Person

You should be...

- **slow to wrath (anger)**. *Ref. James 1:19*

- **swift (quick) to hear, slow to speak**. *Ref. James 1:19*

- **doers of the word,** and **not hearers only**. *Ref. James 1:22-25*

- (doing) that which is **honest**. *Ref. II Corinthians 13:7*

And...

- **(control your tongue)**. *Ref. James 1:26*

- (know that) God resisteth the proud, but giveth grace to the **humble**. *Ref. James 4:6*

- **steal no more** (him that stole): **but rather let him labour,** working with his hands the **things which is good**, that he **may have to give to him that needeth**. *Ref. Ephesians 4:28*

- **seek ye first the Kingdom of God, and his righteousness.** Ref. Matthew 6:33

- **put on...as the elect of God...bowels of mercies,** kindness, humbleness of mind, meekness, longsuffering. *Ref. Col. 3:12*

- **put on charity (love), which is the bond of perfectness.** *Ref. Col. 3:14*

- **purge (yourself)** from (sin), he shall be a vessel unto honour, sanctified, and meet **(prepared)** for the master's use and prepared unto every good work. *Ref. II Timothy 2:21*

- the God of peace...make you **perfect in every good work to do his will,** working in you that which is **well-pleasing in his sight**. *Ref. Hebrews 13:20, 21*

You should...

- **let your light so shine before men**, that they may see your good works, and glorify your Father which is in heaven. *Ref. Matthew 5:16*

- doest alms **(giving)...in secret**: and thy Father which seeth in secret shall reward thee openly. *Ref. Matthew 6:3, 4*

- when thou **prayest**, enter into thy closet **(private place)...pray to thy Father in secret;** and thy Father which seeth in secret shall reward thee openly. *Ref. Matthew 6:6*

- let the **peace of God rule in your (heart)**. *Ref. Colossians 3:15*

- let the **word of Christ dwell in you** richly in all wisdom. *Ref. Colossians 3:16*

- whatsoever things are **true**, whatsoever things *are* **honest**, whatsoever things *are* **just**, whatsoever things *are* **pure**, whatsoever things *are* **lovely**, whatsoever things *are* **of good report**...think on these things. *Ref. Philippians 4:8*

- **follow** after righteousness, godliness, faith, love, patience, meekness. *Ref. I Timothy 6:11*

- put on the **new man,** which after God is created **in righteousness** and **true holiness**. *Ref. Ephesians 4:24*

- **add** to your **faith** virtue (righteousness); and to virtue **(righteousness)** knowledge; and to **knowledge** temperance (self-control); and to temperance **(self-control)** patience; and to **patience** godliness; and to **godliness** brotherly kindness; and to **brotherly kindness** charity **(love)**.
  *For if these **be in you** and bound (stay), they make you that ye shall neither be barren nor unfruitful in the knowledge of our Lord Jesus Christ. *Ref. II Peter 1:5-8*

- **stand (be established)**...having...truth...righteousness...gospel of peace...the shield of faith...salvation, and the sword of the Spirit, which is the word of God: Praying always with all prayer and supplication in the Spirit. *Ref. Ephesians 6:14-18*

You should not...

- **speak evil** of no man. *Ref. Titus 3:2*

- **Offend** ... in word. James 3:2

- **out of the same mouth...blessing and cursing.** *Ref. James 3:10*

- **(let)** fornication, and all uncleanness, or covetousness (greed)... **be once named among you, as becometh saints**; Neither filthiness, nor foolish talking, nor jesting (clowning or teasing). *Ref. Ephesians 5:3, 4*

- Let...**corrupt communication** proceed out of your mouth, but that which is good to the use of edifying, that it may minister grace unto the hears. *Ref. Ephesians 4:29*

- **judge**...that ye be not judged. *Ref. Matthew 7:1*

- alms **(give)** before men, **to be seen** of them...have **(receive)** glory of men. *Ref. Matthew 6:1-4, 5-8*

- **(pray) as the hypocrites**...standing in the synagogues and in the corners of the streets, that they may be seen of men. *Ref. Matthew 6:5*

- **(pray using)...vain repetitions,** as the heathens do: for they think that they will be heard for their much speaking. *Ref. Matthew 6:7*

- **Lay...up** for yourself **treasures upon earth**...lay up for yourselves treasures in heaven...for where your treasure is, there will your heart be also. *Ref. Matthews 6:19-21*

- **be** weary **(troubled) in doing well**, for in due season we shall reap, if we faint not (don't give up). *Ref. Galatians 6:9*

Know that...

- the **works of the flesh** are...*adultery, fornication, uncleanness, lasciviousness, idolatry, witchcraft, hatred, variance, emulations,* *wrath, strife, seditions, heresies, envying, murders, drunkenness, revelings,* and such like. *Ref. Galatians 5:19-21*

- the **fruit of the Spirit** is *love, joy, peace, longsuffering, gentleness, goodness, faith, meekness, (and) temperance (self-control).* *Ref. Gal. 5:22, 23*

- the **kingdom of God** is...*righteousness,* and *peace,* and *joy* in the Holy Ghost. *Ref. Romans 14:17*

- it is God which worketh in you both **to will** and **do his good pleasure.** *Ref. Phil.2:13*

Know the effect!

- Every tree is known by his own fruit. **A good man** out of the goodness of his heart **bringeth forth that which is good** of the abundance of the heart his mouth speaketh. *Ref. Luke 6:44, 45*

- **Every idle (careless) word** that men shall speak, they shall **give account** thereof in the day of judgement. *Ref. Matthews 12:36*

- **By thy words** thou shalt be **justified.** *Ref. Matthews 12:37*

- God will **render** to every man **according to his deeds**...there is no respect of persons with God. *Ref. Romans 2:6,11*

- **Ye are the salt of the earth.** *Ref. Matthews 5:13*

- **Ye are the light of the world**...let your light so shine before men, that they may see your good works, and glorify your Father which is in heaven. *Ref. Matthews 5:14, 16*

You must also know that...

- **nothing** from without a man, that **entering into him can defile him**: but the **things which come out of him**, those are they that **defile the man**.

  For **from within, out of the heart of men**, proceed evil thoughts, adulteries, fornications, murders, thefts, covetousness, wicked-ness, deceit, lasciviousness, an evil eye, blasphemy, pride, foolish-ness: **All these evil things come from within, and defile the man.** *Ref. Mark 7:15, 21-23*

- **ye...are** the **temple of God,** and that the Spirit of God dwelleth in you. *Ref. I Corinthians 3:16, 17*

- no man say when he is tempted, I am tempted of God: for God cannot be tempted with evil, neither tempteth he any man: But every **man is tempted**, when he is **drawn away** of his own lust **(desires)**, and enticed **(by his appetite, exposures, and peer pres-sures)**. Then when **lust hath conceived, it bringeth forth sin**: and sin, when it is finished, bringeth forth death. *Ref. James 1:12-15*

- **they that are Christ's have crucified the flesh** with the affections and lusts (worldly desires). *Ref. Galatians 5:24*

- if a man **think himself to be something**, when he is nothing, he deceiveth himself. *Ref. Galatians 6:3, 4*

- whatsoever a **man soweth**, that shall **he also reap**. For he that soweth to his flesh shall of the flesh reap corruption; but **he that soweth to the Spirit** shall of the Spirit **reap life everlasting**. *Ref. Galatians 6:7, 8*

Young men...

- be sober minded **(clear-headed)**...shewing thyself a pattern of **good works**: in doctrine shewing **uncorruptness**, gravity **(seriousness)**, sincerity **(genuineness)**, **sound speech (words)**, that cannot be condemned. *Ref. Titus 2:6-8*

Women...

- **adorn themselves** in **modest** apparel **(clothing)**, with shame-facedness and sobriety **(dignity)**; not with broided hair, or gold, or pearls, or costly array; but **(which is becometh of women professing godliness) with good works**. *Ref. I Timothy 2:9, 10*

Aged men...

- be sober **(clear-headed)**, grave **(serious)**, temperate **(calm)**, **sound in faith, in** charity **(love)**, in **patience**. *Ref. Titus 2:2*

Aged women...

- (behave) **as becometh holiness, not false accusers, not given to much wine, teachers of good things;** That they **may teach the young women** to be sober (clear-headed), to **love their husbands**, to **love their children**, to be **discreet,** chaste **(faithful), keepers at home, good, obedient to their own husbands**, that the word of God be not blasphemed. *Ref. Titus 2:3-5*

What Does God Expect and Require of Christians?

According to New Testament Scriptures

Live a Godly Life

What Does God Expect and Require of Christians?
Live a Godly Life

Live...

- **(honest)** among the Gentiles (unbelievers)...they may by your good works, which they shall behold, glorify God. *Ref. I Peter 2:12*

- **without** covetousness **(greed)**; and be **content** with such things as you have what you have. *Ref. Hebrews 13:5*

- **a quiet and peaceable life in all godliness and honesty** (all that are in authority). *Ref. I Timothy 2:2*

- **as children of light**: (For the fruit of the Spirit is in all goodness and righteousness and truth;) **Proving what is acceptable unto the Lord**. *Ref. Ephesians 5:8-10*

- **honestly toward them that are without.** *Ref. I Thessalonians 4:12*

- **ye in him (Jesus Christ):** Rooted and built up in him, and established in the faith. *Ref. Colossians 2:6,7*

- **not after the flesh, but after the Spirit**...they that are in the flesh cannot please God. *Ref. Romans 8:4, 8*

- **worthy of the Lord**...being **fruitful in every good**, and **increasing in the knowledge of God**. *Ref. Colossians 1:10, 11*

- **as dear children...in love.** *Ref. Ephesians 5:2*

- soberly **(earnestly), righteously, and godly** in this present world. *Ref. Titus 2:12*

You should...

- **pray** without ceasing. *Ref. I Thessalonians 5:17*

- in every thing **give thanks**. *Ref. I Thessalonians 5:18*

- **hold fast to that which is good.** *Ref. I Thessalonians 5:21*

- abstain **(refrain) from all appearance of evil.** *Ref. I Thessalonians 5:22*

- **put off concerning** the **former** conversation **(living)** of the old man, which is corrupt according to the deceitful lusts (desires). *Ref. Ephesians 4:22*

- **put on** the **new man**, which is created in **righteousness** and **true holiness.** *Ref. Ephesians 4:24*

- Seek those things which are above...**set your affections on things above**, not on things on this earth. *Ref. Col. 3:1, 2*

- **say, if the Lord will**, I will live, and do this, or that. *Ref. James 4:15*

- **denying ungodliness** and **worldly lusts (desires), we should live soberly, righteously, and godly** in this present world. *Ref. Titus 2:12*

- **present your (body) a living sacrifice, holy, acceptable unto God,** *which is* your reasonable service. *Ref. Romans 12:1*

You should be...

- his **(God's) workmanship,** created in Jesus Christ **unto good works.** *Ref. Ephesians 2:10*

- zealous **(passionate)** of **good works.** *Ref. Titus 2:14*

- **(following) after <u>righteousness, godliness, faith, love, patience,</u> and <u>meekness</u>.** *Ref. I Timothy 6:11*

- **followers of God,** as dear children **(sons and daughters of the Father).** *Ref. Ephesians 5:1*

- **transformed by the renewing of your mind** – that you **may prove what is good** and **acceptable and perfect will of God.** *Ref. Romans 12:2*

- **gentle unto all** *men*, apt (able, ready) to teach, patient, in meekness instructing those that oppose themselves... *that* they may recover themselves out of the snare of the devil, who are taken captive by him at his will. *Ref. II Timothy 2:24-26*

- **holy in all manner of conversation (living).** *Ref. I Peter 1:15*

- **(speaking)** always **with grace**, seasoned with salt, that ye may know how ye ought to answer every man. *Ref. Colossians 4:6*

Jessie Clark

You should do...

- **all** to the glory of God. *Ref. I Corinthians 10:31*

- **All things without murmurings (complaining) and disputing**...that ye may be blameless and harmless...in the midst of this crooked and perverse generation – **among whom ye shine as lights in the world**. *Ref. Philippians 2:14-16*

- **whatever ... in word or deed** ... (do) in the name of the Lord Jesus, giving thanks to God and the Father by him. *Ref. Colossians 3:17*

- **and will do the things** which are **commanded of you**. *Ref. II Thessalonians 3:4*

You should not...

- **let sin...(rule, control)...your mortal body**, that you should obey it in the lusts (desires). *Ref. Romans 6:12*

- **yield (surrender)**...instruments of unrighteousness...but...**of righteousness unto God.** *Ref. Romans 6:13*

- **be...conformed to this world**. *Ref. Romans 12:2*

- **(be) ignorant to God's righteousness**...(not) establish...own righteousness. *Ref. Romans 10:3*

- **lust (desire) after evil things**. *Ref. I Corinthians 10:6*

- **be...unequally yoked together with unbelievers:** for what fellowship hath righteousness with unrighteousness...come out from among them, be ye separate. *Ref. II Corinthians 6:14, 17*

- **walk (live) as other Gentiles (unbelievers) walk...understanding darkened**, being alienated from the life of God through the ignorance that is in them, because of the **blindness of their heart.** *Ref. Ephesians 4:17, 18*

Know that...

- where **your treasures is**, there will your heart be also. *Ref. Matthews 6:21*

- the **just shall live by faith**. *Ref. Romans 1:17*

- **to him that knoweth to do good**, and doeth it not, to him it is sin. *Ref. James 4:17*

- **he that doeth wrong** shall receive for the wrong which he hath done. *Ref. Colossians 3:25*

- **we brought nothing into this world**, and it is certain we can carry nothing out. *Ref. I Timothy 6:7*

- **tribulation (troubles)** work patience; and **patience,** experience; and **experience,** hope; and **hope make you not ashamed.** *Ref. Romans 5:3-5*

- **it is God which worketh in you** both to will and to do his good pleasure. *Ref. Philippians 2:13*

Know the work of the flesh and Spirit

- They that are **in the flesh cannot please God.** *Ref. Romans 8:8*

- **Walk (live) in the spirit**, and ye shall **not fulfil the lust of the flesh.** For the flesh lusteth against the spirit, and the spirit against the flesh: and **these are contrary the one to the other**: so that ye cannot do the things that ye would. *Ref. Galatians 5:16, 17*

- The **works of the flesh...**adultery, fornication, uncleanness, lasciviousness, idolatry, witchcraft, hatred, variance, emulations, wrath, strife, seditions, heresies, envying, murders, drunkenness, reveling, and such like. *Ref. Galatians 5:19-21*

- The **fruit of the Spirit** is love, joy, peace, longsuffering, gentleness, goodness, faith, Meekness, temperance: against such there is no law. *Ref. Galatians 5:22, 23*

- The **fruit of the Spirit** is in **all goodness and righteousness and truth;** Proving what is acceptable unto the Lord. *Ref. Ephesians 5:9, 10*

What Does God Expect and Require of Christians?

According to New Testament Scriptures

Spiritual Growth/Maturity/ Transformation

What Does God Expect and Require of Christians?
Spiritual Growth/Maturity/ Transformation

Unfortunately, for many Christians, growing and maturing spiritually is not even a thought or desire. It is not something that is talked about, taught much, or given much attention to. God expects, and requires us, to grow and be transformed into a spiritually mature child of his.

Why is it important that you grow/mature spiritually?

1. It's what the Lord expects and requires of you.

2. Your life will influence others in a godly way and draw others to God.

3. It will help you to know God and his will for you.

4. It will give you spiritual discernment (an ability to know what's of God and what's not).

5. You won't be so easy influenced by people and things that are ungodly.

6. You will be better able to know and understand scriptures.

7. If you don't you run the risk of being – deceived, misinformed, misled, controlled and manipulated and **YOU WON'T EVEN KNOW IT**.

What does spiritual growth/maturity look like?

It is not just what you do or say –

Your spiritual growth/maturity is evident in the person you have become (or are becoming) and the life that you are living. It is made known by your **love, joy, peace, patience, faith, goodness, meekness, gentleness,** and **self-control**.

The light of God in you becomes so illuminating that it's recognized by everyone that you interact with (your spouse, family members, the church, the community, people on your job, and the likes).

People see less of you and more of God in you –

How do you grow/mature and make this transformation?

You will need to...

- have a **sincere desire** to grow/mature and be transformed spiritually.

- become more **fully dependent** on God.

- get help from the **church** – a place where you can learn and understand God's word, get encouragement, and have godly fellowship.

- get help from **others** – people that will encourage you, godly friends and supporters – people who are sincerely concerned about your spiritual wellbeing.

- personally, **study scriptures** more to know and understand God's word and his will.

- have more **prayer** and **quiet devotional time**.

- **involve yourself** in that which is more helpful to your spiritual growth/maturity – such as TV programs, movies, books, places you go, people you associate with, conversations you have, and the likes.

- be **ready** to **accept the truth** – there are some that even when presented with the truth chose to deny it, ignore it, outright refuse to accept it, or just go along with what is considered to be acceptable and popular. However, there may be some that haven't grown enough spiritually to recognize truth when they see or hear it.

It's expected and required of you

- God of hope fill you with all joy and peace in believing, **that ye may abound (grow) in hope**, through the power of the Holy Ghost. *Ref. Romans 15:13*

- As ye abound **(grow) in every***thing, in* faith, and utterance, and knowledge, and in all diligence...*see* that ye abound **(grow)** in this grace also. *Ref. II Corinthians 8:7*

- Leaving the principles of the doctrine of Christ, let us go on unto **perfection (maturity)**. *Ref. Hebrews 6:1*

- As newborn babes desire the sincere milk of the word, **that ye may (grow)**. *Ref. I Peter 2:2*

- (Jesus is the vine), ye *are* the branches: He that abide in (Jesus), and (Jesus) in him, **the same bringeth forth much fruit (growth).** *Ref. John 15:5*

- For when the time ye ought to be teachers, ye have need that one teach you...and are become such as have need of milk, and not of strong meat. For every one that useth milk is unskillful in the word of righteousness: for **he is a babe**. But strong meat belongeth to them that are of full age **(spiritually mature)**. *Ref. Hebrews 5:12,13*

- Seek that ye may excel **(grow)** to the **edifying (improving) of the church**. *Ref. I Corinthians 14:12*

- Gave some, apostles; and some, prophets; and some, evangelists; and some, pastors, and teachers; **For the (perfecting) of saints**, for the work of the ministry, for the edifying **(improving)** of the **body of Christ**...unto a perfect man...**no more children,** tossed to and fro, and carried about with every wind of doctrine (teaching) by the **sleight of men**, and cunning craftiness (deceitfulness), whereby they lie and **wait to deceive**. *Ref. Ephesians 4:11-14*

Help Provided

- Whatsoever things were **written aforetime** were **written for our learning**, that we through patience and comfort of the scriptures might have hope. *Ref. Romans 15:4*

- God of hope fill you with all joy and peace in believing, that ye may abound (grow) in hope, **through the power of the Holy Ghost**. *Ref. Romans 15:13*

- We have received, not the spirit of the world, but the **spirit which is of God**; that we might know the things that are freely given to us of God. Which things also we speak, not in the words which man's wisdom teacheth, but which the **Holy Ghost teacheth**, comparing spiritual things with spiritual. *Ref. I Corinthians 2:12, 13*

- He gave some, **apostles**; and some, **prophets**; and some, **evangelists**; and some, **pastors** and **teachers**; For the **perfecting of the saints**, for the work of the ministry, for the edifying (improvement) of the body of Christ. *Ref. Ephesians 4:11, 12*

- The whole body fitly joined together ... **every joint supplieth**, according to the effectual working in the measure of every part, make increase of the body unto the edifying of itself in love. *Ref. Ephesians 4:15, 16*

- **All scripture** is given by inspiration God, and is profitable for doctrine (teaching), for reproof (reprimand), for (correction), for (instruction in righteousness): that the man of God may be perfect, thoroughly furnished unto all good works. *Ref. II Timothy 3:16, 17*

- Be sober (clearheaded), be vigilant (attentive); because your adversary the devil, as a roaring lion, walk about, seeking whom he may devour: resist in the faith, knowing that the same **afflictions**... **after that ye have suffered a while**, make you perfect, stablish, strengthen, settle *you. Ref. I Peter 5:8-10*

- But the **Comforter**, which is the **Holy Ghost**, whom the Father will send in my name, he shall **teach you all things**, and **bring all things to your remembrance**. *Ref. John 14:26*

What Does God Expect and Require of Christians?

According to New Testament Scriptures

The Church

What Does God Expect and Require of Christians?
The Church

- The **church**, which is **his** (Jesus Christ) **body**. *Ref. Ephesians 1:22, 23*

- The **house of God**, which is the **church of the living God**. *Ref. I Timothy 3:15*

- He might present it to himself a **(glorious church) not having spot, or wrinkles, or any such thing**...that it should be **holy and without blemish**. *Ref. Ephesians 5:27*

- **Saints...we should be holy and without blame** before him in love: having predestinated us unto the **adoption of children** by Jesus Christ to himself, according to the good pleasure of his will. *Ref. Ephesians 1:1, 4, 5*

- Not forsaking the **assembling of ourselves together...** but exhorting **(encouraging) one another**. *Ref. Hebrews 10:25*

Pure religion...is this, **to visit** *the fatherless and widows in their afflictions (troubles), and to* **keep** *himself unspotted from the world. Ref. James 1:27*

Members of One Body

- For as we have **many members in one body**, all members have not the same office...being many, are **one body in Christ**. *Ref. Romans 12:4, 5*

- God set the **members every one of them in the body**, as it hath pleased him. *Ref. I Corinthians 12:18*

- God hath **tempered the body together**...that **members should have the same care one for another** ... whether one member suffer, all the members suffer with it; or one member be honored, all the members rejoice. *Ref. I Corinthians 12:24-26*

- From whom the **whole body fitly joined together**...**every joint supplieth**, according to the effectual working in the measure of every part, **make increase of the body unto the edifying (improving) of itself in love**. *Ref. Ephesians 4:16*

The Beginning Church

- They that gladly **received his word** were **baptized**: and the same day there were added unto them about three thousand souls. *Ref. Acts 2:41*

- They **continued** stedfastly in the apostles' doctrine **(teachings)** and **fellowship, breaking bread,** and in **prayers**. *Ref. Acts 2:42*

- Many **wonders** and **signs** were done by the apostles. *Ref. Acts 2:43*

- **All that believed** were together and had **all things common**; And **sold their possessions and goods**, and **parted them to all men**, as every man had need. *Ref. Acts 2:44, 45*

- They, continuing **daily** with one accord (same mindset) in the temple, and **breaking bread** from house to house...**praising God, and having favour with all people**. *Ref. Acts 2:46, 47*

- **The Lord added** to the church daily such as should be saved. *Ref. Acts 2:47*

- The multitude of them that believed were of **one heart** and of **one soul: neither said** any of them that ought of the **things which he possessed was his own; but they had all things common.** *Ref. Acts 4:32*

- **Neither** was there any among them that **lacked**; for as many as were possessors of lands or houses sold them, and brought the prices of the things that were sold, and laid them at the apostles' feet: and **distribution** was made **unto every man according as he had need**. *Ref. Acts 4:34,35*

- **Daily** in the **temple**, and in **every house**, they (apostles) ceased not to **teach** and **preached Jesus Christ**. *Ref. Acts 5:42*

Spiritual Gifts

- **Gifts differing** according to the grace that is given to us, whether **prophecy**, *let us prophesy* according to the proportion of faith; Or **ministry**, *let us wait* on *our* ministering: or he that **teacheth**, on teaching; Or he that **exhorteth**, on exhortation: **he that giveth**, *let* *him do it* with simplicity; **he that ruleth**, with diligence; **he that sheweth mercy**, with cheerfulness. *Ref. Romans 12:6-8*

- There are **diversities of gifts**, but the **same Spirit**.

  There are **differences of administrations**, but the **same Lord**.

  There are **diversities of operations**, but it is the **same God** which **worketh all in all**.

  But the manifestation **(demonstration) of the Spirit is given to every man to profit withal (all)**. *Ref. I Corinthians 12:4-7*

- For to one is given by the Spirit the **word of wisdom;** to another the **word of knowledge**...to another **faith**...to another **gift of healing**...to another **working of miracles**...to another **prophecy**...to another **discerning of spirits**...to another divers **(various) kinds of tongues**...to another **the interpretation of tongues**...dividing to every man severally as he will. *Ref. I Corinthians 12:8-11*

Roles God placed in the Church

- God hath set some in the church...**first apostles, secondarily prophets, thirdly teachers,** after that **miracle (miracle workers), then gifts of healings, helps, governments, diversities (various) of tongues.** *Ref. I Corinthians 12:28*

- He gave some **apostles; and some, prophets; and some, evangelists; and some, pastors, and teachers; (why?)** For the <u>perfecting of the saints</u>, for the <u>work of the ministry</u>, for the <u>edifying of the body of Christ</u> – **(why?)**...that we henceforth **be no more children**, tossed to and fro, and carried about with every wind of doctrine (teaching) by the sleight of men, and cunning craftiness whereby they lie in wait to deceive. *Ref. Ephesians 4:11-14*

Bishop

- A bishop then must be **blameless**, the **husband of one wife**, vigilant **(alert), sober, of good behavior, given to hospitality, apt to teach, not given to wine, no** striker **(attacker), not greedy of** filthy lucre **(gain),** but **patient, not a brawler, not** covetous **(greedy),** one that **rule well his own house,** having his children in subjection with all gravity (dignity), (for if a man knows not how to rule his own house, how shall he take care of the church of God?) **Not a novice,** being lifted up with pride he falls into the condemnation of the devil. Moreover, he must have **a good report of them which are without**; lest he fall into reproach and the snare of the devil. *Ref. I Timothy 3:2-7*

- A Bishop must be **blameless,** as the steward **(overseer)** of God; **not self-willed, not soon angry, not given to wine, no** striker **(attacker), not given to** filthy lucre **(gain),** but a **lover of hospitality,** a **lover of good men, sober, just, holy,** temperate **(having self-control).** *Ref. Titus 1:7, 8*

Elders

- When they had **ordained them Elders in every church,** and had prayed with fasting, they commended them to the Lord, on whom they believed. *Ref. Acts 14:23*

- Take heed therefore unto yourselves, and to all the flock, over which the Holy Ghost hath made you **overseers, to feed the church of God.** *Ref. Acts 20:28*

- **Ye ought to support the weak,** and to **remember** the words of the Lord Jesus, how he said, **it is more blessed to give than to receive.** *Ref. Acts 20:35*

- Let the **elders that rule well** be counted worthy of double honor (respect, esteem) especially they who labor in the word and doctrine (teaching). *Ref. I Timothy 5:17*

- **Ordain** elders in every city, as I had appointed thee: if any be **blameless,** the **husband of one wife,** having **faithful children** not accused of riot or unruly. *Ref. Titus 1:5, 6*

- Elders which are among you I exhort...**feed the flock of God** which is among you, taking the **oversight** thereof, **not** by constraint **(control),** but willingly; **not for** filthy lucre **(gain),** but of a ready mind, **neither as being lords over** *God's* **heritage** but **being examples to the flock.** *Ref. I Peter 5:1-3*

Deacons

- Be grave **(sincere), not double-tongued, not given to much wine, not greedy of** filthy lucre **(gain), holding the mystery of the faith** in a pure conscience...**found blameless** – Even so must their **wives** be **grave, not slanderers, sober, faithful in all things...**

  Let the deacons be the husbands of one wife, ruling their children and their own houses **well.** *Ref. I Timothy 3:8-13*

7 Men Chosen to Relieve the Apostles

What was the issue?

- When the number of the disciples was multiplied, there arose a murmuring **(grumbling)** of the Grecians against the Hebrews, **(why)** because **their widows were neglected** in the daily ministration (care). *Ref. Acts 6:1*

Why couldn't the 12 meet the needs of this issue?

- Then the twelve called the multitude of the disciples...and said, **it is not reason that we** (apostles) **should leave the word of God, and serve tables ...we will give ourselves continually to prayer, and to the ministry of the word.** *Ref. Acts 6:2, 4*

Who was asked to find help?

- **Brethren**, look ye out among you seven (7) men...whom we (apostles) may appoint over this business. *Ref. Acts 6:3*

What were the qualifications?

- Seven (7) men **of honest report**, full of the **Holy Ghost** and **wisdom**. *Ref. Acts 6:3*

Who did they choose?

- They chose **Stephen**, a man full of faith and of the Holy Ghost, and **Philip**, and **Prochorus**, and **Nicanor**, and **Timon**, and **Parmenas**, and **Nicolas**...whom they (disciples) set before the (apostles): and when they had prayed, they laid their hands on them. *Ref. Acts 6:5, 6*

Preaching and Teaching

- They which **preach the gospel** should **live of the gospel**. *Ref. I Corinthians 9:14*

- **Wheresoever this gospel is preached** throughout the whole world, this also that she hath done shall be spoken of for a memorial of her. *Ref. Mark 14:9*

- **Teach no other doctrine,** neither give heed to fables (stories) and endless genealogies, which minister questions, rather than godly edifying. *Ref. I Timothy 1:3, 4*

- If any man...consent not to wholesome words, *even* the **words of our Lord Jesus Christ**, and to the doctrine **(teaching) which is according to godliness**; he is proud, knowing nothing...supposing that gain is godliness: from such withdraw thyself. *Ref. I Timothy 6:3-5*

- When I (Paul) preach the gospel, I may make the gospel of Christ **without charge**, that I abuse not my power in the gospel. *Ref. I Corinthians 9:18*

- **Study to shew thyself approved unto God...rightly dividing the word of truth**. *Ref. II Timothy 2:15*

- **Avoid profane** and vain **(useless) babblings**. *Ref. I Timothy 6:20*

- Strive not about **words to no profit**. *Ref. II Timothy 2:14*

- **We speak; not as pleasing men, but God, which trieth our hearts**... **neither at any time used we flattering words**... **neither sought glory of men**. *Ref. I Thessalonians 2:4-6*

- I (Paul)...came not with **excellency of speech (words)** or **of wisdom**... for I determined not to know any thing among you, save Jesus Christ, and him crucified...and my speech and preaching was **not** with **enticing words of man's wisdom**, but in demonstration of the spirit and of power:

  that (their) faith should not stand in the wisdom of men, but in the power of God. *Ref. I Corinthians 2:1-5*

Giving (the beginning church)

- **Neither was there any among them that lacked**; for as many as were possessors of lands or houses sold them...**distribution was made unto every man according as he had need**. *Ref. Acts 4:34, 35*

- Sold their possessions and goods, and parted them to all men, **as every man had need**. *Ref. Acts 2:45*

Giving

- **Give to him that asketh of thee**, and from **him that would borrow of thee turn not away**. *Ref. Matthews 5:42*

- **That alms (giving) should be in secret**: and the Father which seeth in secret himself shall reward you openly. *Ref. Matthews 6:4*

- There came a certain **poor widow,** and she threw in two mites... hath cast more in, than all they which have cast into the treasury: for all they did cast in of their abundance; but she of her want did **cast in all that she had, even all her living**. *Ref. Mark 12:42-44*

- (Elders) **support the weak,** and remember the words of the Lord Jesus, how he said, **it is more blessed to give than receive**. *Ref. Acts 20:35*

- **Give**, and **it shall be given unto you**; good measure, pressed down, and shaken together, and running over, shall men give into your bossom. For with the same measure that ye mete (give) withal it shall be measured to you again. *Ref. Luke 6:38*

- Concerning the **collection <u>for the saints</u>...*upon the first day of the week*** let everyone of you lay by him in store, as God hath prospered him, that there be no gatherings **when I (Paul) come**. *Ref. I Corinthians 16:1, 2*

- They have addicted themselves to the <u>**ministry of the saints**</u>...**for that which was lacking on your part they have supplied.** *Ref. I Corinthians 16:15, 18*

- For if there be first **a willing mind**, *it is* accepted according to that a man hath, *and* not according to that he hath not. *Ref. II Corinthians 8:12*

- Your abundance *may be a supply* for **their want**, that their abundance also may be *a supply* for **your want**...he that *had gathered* much had nothing over; and **he that *had gathered* little had no lack**. *Ref. II Corinthians 8:14,15*

- The **ministering to the saints**, it is superfluous (unnecessary) for me to write to you...I boast of you to them of Macedonia. *Ref. II Corinthians 9:1, 2*

- He which **soweth sparingly** shall **reap** also **sparingly**; and he which **soweth bountifully** shall reap **also bountifully**. *Ref. II Corinthians 9:6*

- Every man according as he purposeth in his heart, **let him give (to the saints)**; not grudgingly, or of necessity: **for God love a cheerful giver.** *Ref. II Corinthians 9:7*

- God is able to make all grace abound toward you...**always having all sufficiency in all things.** *Ref. II Corinthians 9:8*

- This service not only supplieth the **want of the saints,** but is abundant also by **many thanksgivings unto God**. *Ref. II Corinthians 9:12*

- They **(saints)** glorify God...**for your liberal (generous) distribution** unto them, and unto all men. *Ref. II Corinthians 9:13*

- If thou wilt be perfect, go and sell that thou hast, and **give to the poor**. *Ref. Matthews 19:21*

- He that hath two coats, let him **impart to him that hath none**; and he that hath meat, let him do likewise. *Ref. Luke 3:11*

- Zacchaeus...half of my goods I **give to the poor**. *Ref. Luke 19:8*

- Every man according to their ability, determined to **send relief (help)** unto the **brethren** which dwelt in Judaea. *Ref. Acts 11: 29*

- Macedonia and Achaia to make a certain contribution **for the poor saints** which are at Jerusalem. *Ref. Romans 15:26*

- Him that stole steal no more: but rather let him labour, working with his hands the things which is good, that he may have to **give to him that needeth**. *Ref. Ephesians 4:28*

- If a **brother or sister** be **naked**, and **destitute of daily food**, and one of you say unto them, depart in peace, be ye warmed and filled; notwithstanding ye give them not those things which are needful to the body; what doth it profit? *Ref. James 2:15,16*

- Whoso hath this world's good, and seeth **his brother have need**, and shutteth up his bowels of compassion from him, how dwelleth the love of God in him. *Ref. I John 3:17*

The Lord's Supper

- The **twelve apostles** were with **Jesus** ... I (Jesus) have desired to eat this **passover** with you before I suffer...he took the **cup**, and gave thanks, and said, take this, and divide *it* among yourselves ...and he took **bread**, and gave thanks, and brake *it*, and gave unto them, saying, **this is my body which is given for you: this do in**

remembrance of me...this **cup** *is* the **new testament in my blood, which is shed for you**. *Ref. Luke 22:14-20*

The problem that arose taking the Lord's Supper

- When you come together in the church, I hear that there be divisions among you... when you come together therefore into one place, *this* is not to eat the Lord's supper.

  For in eating **everyone taketh before *other* his own supper**: and **one is hungry**, and **another is drunken**. What? have you not houses to eat and to drink in? *Ref. I Corinthians 11:18-22*

- Whosoever eat this bread, and drink this cup of the Lord, **unworthily**, shall be **guilty of the body and blood of the Lord**. But let a man **examine himself**, and so let him eat of *that* bread, and drink of *that* cup. For he that eateth and drinketh **unworthily**, eateth and drinketh **damnation to himself**, not discerning the Lord's body. *Ref. I Corinthians 11:27-29*

- For this cause **many *are* weak and sickly among you, and many sleep**. *Ref. I Corinthians 11:30*

- My brethren, **when ye come together to eat, tarry (wait) one for another. And if any man hunger, let him eat at home**; that ye come not together unto condemnation. *Ref. I Corinthians 11:33, 34*

When (troubled, happy, or sick)

- Is any among you are **afflicted (troubled)?** let him **pray**. *Ref. James 5:13*

- Is any **merry** – let him **sing psalms**. *Ref. James 5:13*

- If any **sick** among you? let him call for the **elders of the church**; and let them **pray over him**, anointing him with oil in the name of the Lord: And the prayer of faith shall save the sick, and the Lord shall raise him up; and **if he has committed sins, they shall be forgiven him**. *Ref. James 5:14, 15*

What Matters Most

- **Martha** received him into her house. And she had a sister called **Mary**, whch sat at Jesus' feet, and **heard his word**. But **Martha** was cumbered (concerned) **about much serving**, and came to him, and said, Lord, dost thou not care that my sister hath left me to serve alone? Bid her to help me.

- Jesus answered and said unto her, Martha, Martha, thou art **careful** and **troubled about many things**: but one thing is needful: and **Mary hath chosen that good part** (listening to the words of Jesus), which shall not be taken away from her. *Ref. Luke 10:38-42*

Jesus sent them on a mission

- He called his **twelve disciples** together, and gave them **power and authority** over **devils,** and to **cure diseases.** He sent them to **preach** the Kingdom of God, and to **heal the sick**. *Ref. Luke 9:1, 2*

- The Lord appointed other **seventy**...sent them **two by two...into every city and place**...carry no purse, nor scrip, nor shoes: and salute no man by the way... **(heal the sick)** that are therein, and say unto them, **the Kingdom of God is come nigh unto you**. *Ref. Luke 10:1, 4, 9*

- The **seventy** returned...saying...**devils are subject unto us through thy name...I (Jesus) give unto you power to** tread on serpents and scorpions, **and over all the power of the enemy: and nothing shall by any means hurt you**. *Ref. Luke 10:17, 19*

"The Great Commission"

- Unto them **(11 disciples)**...go...**teach** all nations, **baptizing** them in the name of the Father, and of the Son, and of the Holy Ghost: **teaching them to observe all things** whatsoever I have commanded you. *Ref. Matthews 28:16, 19, 20*

- He said unto them **(11 disciples)**, go ye into the world, and **preach the gospel to every creature.** He that believeth and is baptized shall be saved. *Ref. Mark 16:15, 16*

- These **signs shall follow them that believe;** in my name shall they cast out devils; they shall speak with new tongues, they shall take up serpents; and if they drink any deadly thing, it shall not hurt them; they shall lay hands on the sick, and they shall recover. *Ref. Mark 16:17, 18*

- They **(11 disciples)** went forth, and preached **everywhere.** *Ref. Mark 16:20*

- Then opened he their **(11 disciples)** understanding, that they might understand the scriptures...**repentance and remission of sins** should be **preached in his name among all nations,** beginning at Jerusalem. *Ref. Luke 24:45-47*

What Does God Expect and Require of Christians?

According to New Testament Scriptures

Be Aware of and Avoid Harmful Influences

What Does God Expect and Require of Christians?
Be Aware of and Avoid Harmful Influences

Our World/Society

Please know that you must be aware of and avoid ungodly influences in this world/society. We see these ungodly influences in TV programs, movies, video games, social media, music and the likes. They promote and encourage evil, disrespectfulness, inappropriate languages, hatred, sex, violence, and the likes.

These ungodly influences in this world/society comes in many different forms and are sometimes disguised and not so obvious. If you are not mindful of these influences, they will hinder your walk with God. You must pray for spiritual discernment and strength so that you can see them and avoid them.

- **Be not conformed to this world**: but be ye **transformed** by the renewing of your mind, that ye may prove what is that good, and acceptable, and perfect, will of God. *Ref. Romans 12:2*

- Pure religion and undefiled before God...**to keep himself unspotted from the world**. *Ref. James 1:27*

- **In time past ye walked according to the course of this world,**

- according to the prince of the power of the air, the spirit that now worketh in the children of disobedience. *Ref. Ephesians 2:2*

- **For all that is in the world**, the **lust of the flesh**, and the **lust of the eyes**, and the **pride of life**, is not of the Father, but is of the world. *Ref. I John 2:16*

- Whatsoever is born of God **overcometh the world**: and this is the victory that overcometh the world, even our faith. *Ref. I John 5:4*

- For we wrestle not against flesh and blood, but against principalities, against powers, **against the rulers of the darkness of this world**, against spiritual wickedness in high places. *Ref. Ephesians 6:12*

- **Beware** lest **any man spoil you...after the rudiments of the world**, and not after Christ. *Ref. Colossians 2:8*

Church

Unfortunately, you must know that there are churches that can hinder rather than help you, spiritually. These churches function based on man-made traditions that have been passed down from generation to generation and/or serve the interest and motives of man.

These churches have given (and continue to give) Christians a false sense of what church and Christianity is all about. There is an appearance of godliness. Those things that are said and done look and sound godly. It is extremely important that you know what is of God and what is not so that you are not led astray in one of these churches.

Men

There are men that go into pastoring a church as a career, an alternative to a traditional job. They know that they will be well taken care of; paid well and provided perks like a car and housing. For many it's a perfect match for their skill set, so they perform very well in this role.

These men sound believable, convincing, exciting, and persuasive. They are very good at manipulating scriptures so that what's said sounds like truth. Their words and actions are usually championed by others who unknowingly support and encourage their manipulation.

It's so very important that you ask God to give you spiritual discernment so that you know what is of God and what is not.

If you don't, you will be influenced by these men, who are usually charming, smart, polished, funny, and very good talkers.

You run the risk of being – **deceived, misled, misinformed, controlled and manipulated** AND YOU WON'T EVEN KNOW IT.

Teachings and Traditions of Men

- **Why**...are ye **subject to** the ordinances **(rules)**...after the **commandments** and **doctrines of men?** *Ref. Colossians 2:20, 22*

- **Be no more children**, tossed to and fro, and carried about with every wind of doctrine, by the sleight **(deceitfulness) of men.** *Ref. Ephesians 4:14*

- This people honoureth me with *their* lips, but **their heart far from me**... **teaching** *for* **doctrines the commandments of men.**

For laying aside the commandment of God, **ye hold the tradition of men**. *Ref. Mark7:6-8*

- Reject the commandment of God, **that ye may keep your own tradition**... making the word of God of none effect through your traditions. *Ref. Mark 7:9, 13*

- There are many unruly and vain **(aimless) talkers** and **deceivers**... **teaching things which they ought not, for filthy lucre's (greed) sake.**

  Rebuke them sharply...not giving heed to...**commandments of men, that turn from the truth**. They profess that they know God; but in their works (actions) they deny *him. Ref. Titus 1:10-16*

- **Beware** lest any man spoil you through **philosophy and deceit**, **after the traditions of men**, after the rudiments (principles) of the world, and **not after Christ**. *Ref. Colossians 2:8*

Be not servants of men.
I Corinthians 7:23

Deceitful men

- This I say, lest any man should beguile **(charm) you** with **enticing words**. *Ref. Colossians 2:4*

- **Let no man deceive you** with **(useless) words**. *Ref. Ephesians 5:6*

- They that **serve** not our Lord Jesus Christ, but **their own belly**; and **by good words and fair speeches** they **deceive** the hearts of the simple (the innocent, the spiritually immature, the babes in Christ). *Ref. Romans 16:18*

■ Through covetousness (greed) shall they with feigned **(deceitful) words make merchandise of you**. *Ref. II Peter 2:3*

■ Walking (living) after their own lust (desires); and their mouth speaketh **great swelling words,** having men's persons in admiration **(admired by men)**. *Ref. Jude 1:16*

■ Being ignorant of God's righteousness, and going about to **establish their own righteousness,** have not submitted themselves unto the righteousness of God. *Ref. Romans 10:3*

■ Also of your own selves shall men arise, speaking preverse (contradictory) things, **to draw away disciples after them.** *Ref. Acts 20:30*

■ There be some that...would pervert **(misrepresent)** the gospel of Christ. *Ref. Galatians 1:7-12*

■ Evil men and **seducers** shall wax **worse and worse,** deceiving, and being deceived. *Ref. II Timothy 3:13*

■ Beware of false prophets, **which come to you in sheep's clothing,** but inwardly they are ravening wolves. Ye shall know them by their fruits. *Ref. Matthews 7:15, 16*

■ For such are false apostles, deceitful workers, **transforming themselves** into the apostles of Christ...Satan himself is **transformed** into **an angel of light...** his ministers also be **transformed** as the **ministers of righteousness.** *Ref. II Corinthians 11:13-15*

- Ye are they which **justify themselves before men**; but God knows their hearts: for that which is **highly esteemed among men** is abomination (disgrace) in the sight of God. *Ref. Luke 16:15*

- In the **last days** perilous times shall come.

  Men shall be lovers of their own selves, covetous (greedy), boasters, proud, blasphemers, disobedient to parents, unthankful, unholy, without natural affection, trucebreakers, false accusers, incontinent, fierce, despisers of those that are good, traitors, heady, high-minded, lovers of pleasures more than lovers of God; **having a form of godliness,** but denying the power thereof: from such turn away. *Ref. II Timothy 3:1-5*

- They which creep into houses, and **lead captive silly women (burdened) with sins**, led away with divers (various) lust (desires), **ever learning**, and **never able to come to the knowledge of the truth**. *Ref. II Timothy 3:6, 7*

What Does God Expect and Require of Christians?

According to New Testament Scriptures

Be Ready When Jesus Returns

What Does God Expect and Require of Christians?

Be ready when Jesus returns

Signs of his return

- What sign *will there be* when these things shall come to pass... **many shall come in my name**, saying, **I am Christ**; and the time draweth near...**nation shall rise against nation**, and **kingdom against kingdom**: and **great earthquakes**...**famines**, and **pestilences**; and **fearful sights** and **great signs shall there be from heaven**. *Ref. Luke 21:7-11*

- Before all these, they shall...**persecute** *you*, delivering *you* to synagogues, and into prisons...for my name's sake...**ye shall be betrayed** both by parents, and brethren, and kinsfolks, and friends; and *some* of you shall they cause to be put to death. And **ye shall be hated of all men for my name's sake**. *Ref. Luke 21:12-17*

- When you shall see **Jerusalem compassed with armies**, then know that the desolation thereof is nigh...these be the days of vengeance, that all things which are written may be fulfilled. *Ref. Luke 21:20-22*

- **Woe unto them that are with child**, and to them that give suck, in those days! for there shall be great distress in the land, and wrath upon this people. *Ref. Luke 21:23*

- There shall be (signs) **in the sun, and in the moon, and in the stars;** and **upon the earth distress of nations,...the sea and the waves roaring; men's hearts failing them for fear,** and for looking after those things which are coming on the earth: for the **powers of heaven shall be shaken.**

- Then shall they see the **Son of man coming in a cloud** with power and great glory. And **when these things begin to come to pass...your redemption draw nigh.** *Ref. Luke 21:25-28*

Be counted worthy

- **Not everyone** that saith unto me, Lord, Lord, shall enter into the kingdom of heaven; but **he that doeth the will of my Father** which is in heaven. Many will say to me in that day, Lord, Lord, have we not prophesied in thy name? and in thy name have cast out devils? and in thy name done many wonderful works? And then will I profess unto them, I never knew you: depart from me, ye that work iniquity. *Ref. Matthews 7:21-23*

- When Christ...appears, then shall ye also appear with him in glory. Mortify therefore your members...**put off the old man** with his deeds...**put on the new man,** which is renewed in knowledge after the image of him that created him. *Ref. Colossians 3:4-10*

- Know that **holiness, without** which no man shall see the Lord. *Ref. Hebrews 12:14*

- What manner *of persons* **ought ye to be** in *all* holy conversation **(living)** and **godliness...**unto the coming of the day of God. *Ref. II Peter 3:11, 12*

Be found blameless

- To them that are sanctified in Christ Jesus, called *to be* saints... waiting for the coming of our Lord Jesus Christ: Who shall also confirm you unto the end, **that ye may be blameless** in the day of our Lord Jesus Christ. *Ref. I Corinthians 1:2, 5-8*

- The Lord make you to increase and abound in love one toward another, and toward all *men...he may e*stablish your hearts **unblameable in holiness** before God...at the coming of our Lord Jesus Christ with all his saints. *Ref. I Thessalonians 3:12, 13*

- Rejoice evermore. Pray without ceasing. In everything give thanks: for this is the will of God in Christ Jesus concerning you...hold fast that which is good. Abstain from all appearance of evil...I pray God your whole spirit and soul and body be **preserved blameless** unto the coming of our Lord Jesus Christ. *Ref. I Thessalonians 5:16-23*

- Be diligent that you may be found of him in peace, without spot, and **blameless**. *Ref. II Peter 3:14*

Salvation

- **Are there few that be saved?**...strive to enter in at the strait gate: for **many**, I say unto you, **will seek to enter in, and shall not be able**. *Ref. Luke 13:23, 24*

- Once the master...shut to the door, and ye...**knock at the door**, saying, Lord, Lord, **open unto us**; and he shall answer...I know you not whence ye are...we have eaten and drunk in thy presence, and thou hast taught in our streets...he shall say... depart from me, all *ye* workers of iniquity. *Ref. Luke 13:25-27*

- **Now is our salvation nearer than when we believed**...let us...cast off the works of darkness, and let us put on the armor of light. Let us walk (live) honestly...make not provision for the flesh, to *fulfil* the lusts (desires) thereof. *Ref. Romans 13:11-14*

- The **gospel** which **I preached unto you**, which also ye have received, and wherein ye stand; **by which also ye are saved, if ye keep in memory what I preached unto you**, unless you have believed in vain. *Ref. I Cor.15:1, 2*

- That day should overtake you as a thief...let us not sleep, as *do* others...let us...be sober, putting on...**the hope of salvation**. *Ref. I Thessalonians 5:4-8*

- God hath not appointed us to wrath, but **to obtain salvation** by our Lord Jesus Christ, who died for us, that, whether we wake or sleep, we should live together with him. *Ref. I Thessalonians 5:9, 10*

- **Work out your own salvation** with fear and trembling. *Ref. Philippians 2:12*

- For we are made partakers of Christ, **if** we **hold the beginning of our confidence stedfast unto the end**. *Hebrews 3:14*

- **If** the **righteous scarcely be saved**, where shall the ungodly and the sinner appear? *Ref. I Peter 4:18*

- The **grace** of God that bringeth **salvation** hath appeared to all men, teaching us that, denying ungodliness and worldly lusts (desires), **we should live soberly (earnestly), righteously**, and **godly,** in this present world. Looking for the appearing of the great God and our Savior Jesus Christ. *Ref. Titus 2:11-13*

Judgment

- In him we live, and move, and have our being...commandeth all men everywhere to repent...he hath appointed a day, in which **he will judge the world in righteousness** by *that* man (Jesus) whom he hath ordained. *Ref. Acts 17:28-31*

- Who will render to **every man according to his deeds... there is no respect of persons with God**. *Ref. Romans 2:6, 11*

- In the day when **God shall judge the secrets of men** by Jesus Christ according to my gospel. *Ref. Romans 2:16*

- Every knee shall bow to me, and every tongue shall confess to God. So, then **every one of us shall give account of himself to God**. *Ref. Romans 14:11, 12*

- Judge nothing before the time, until the Lord come, who both will **bring to light the hidden things of darkness, and will make manifest the counsels of the hearts**. *Ref. I Corinthians 4:5*

- We must all appear before the **judgment seat of Christ;** that **every one may receive the things done in his body, according to that he hath done, whether it be good or bad**. *Ref. II Corinthians 5:10*

- The time *is come* that **judgment must begin at the house of God...**

  if the **righteous scarcely be saved**, where shall the ungodly and the sinner appear? *Ref. I Peter 4:17, 18*

Be Persistence

- As we have borne the image of the earthy, we shall also bear the image of the heavenly...in a moment, in the twinkling of an eye, at the last trump...and the dead shall be raised incorruptible, and we shall be changed...**be ye steadfast, unmovable, always abounding in the work of the Lord**, forasmuch as ye know that your labor is not in vain in the Lord. *Ref. I Corinthians 15:49, 52, 58*

- Fight the good fight of faith, **lay hold** on eternal life...**Keep *this* commandment without spot, unrebukable, until** the appearing of our Lord Jesus Christ. *Ref. I Timothy 6:12, 14*

- He which has begun a good work in you will perform *it* **until the day of Jesus Christ**...that ye may be **sincere and without offence** till the day of Christ; **being filled with the fruits of righteousness.** *Ref. Philippians 1:6, 9-11*

- We ought to **give the more earnest heed** to the things which we have heard, lest **at any time we should let them slip.** For If the word spoken by angels was stedfast (certain), and every transgression (sin) and disobedience received a just reward. How shall we escape, if we neglect so great salvation. *Ref. Hebrews 2:1-3*

- We desire that every one of you **do shew the same diligence (persistence)** to the **full assurance of hope unto the end**: that ye **be not slothful**, but followers of them who through faith and patience inherit the promises. *Ref. Hebrews 6:11, 12*

Be Watchful

- Be...ready...**for the Son of man come at an hour when ye think not**. *Ref. Luke 12:40*

- We which are alive *and* remain unto the coming of the Lord shall not prevent them which are asleep. **The Lord himself shall descend from heaven** with a shout, with the voice of the archangel, and with the trump of God: and the dead in Christ shall rise first: Then we which are alive *and* remain shall be caught up together with them in the clouds, to meet the Lord in the air. *Ref. I Thessalonians 4:15-17*

- **The day of the Lord so cometh as a thief in the night**. For when they say, peace and safety; then sudden destruction cometh upon them...they shall not escape. *Ref. I Thessalonians 5:2, 3*

- Be not soon shaken in mind, or be troubled, neither by spirit, nor by word...**as that the day of Christ is at hand**. *Ref. II Thessalonians 2:2*

- Be sober **(alert)**, and hope to the end for the grace that is to be brought unto you at the revelation of Jesus Christ; as obedient children, not fashioning (adapting) yourselves according to the former lusts (desires) in your ignorance...**be ye holy in all manner of conversation (living)**. *Ref. I Peter 1:13-15*

- The end of all things is at hand: be...sober **(alert)**, and **(watch)** unto **(prayer)**. *Ref. I Peter 4:7*

Separation when Jesus returns

- He that **soweth** the good seed is the **Son of man**; The field is the world; The <u>good seed</u> are the **children of the kingdom**...<u>tares</u> are the **children of the wicked *one***; the enemy that sowed them is the devil; the **harvest is the end of the world**; and the **reapers are the angels**...the tares are gathered and burned in the fire; so shall it be in the end of this world. *Ref. Matthews 13:37-40*

- The Son of man shall **send forth his angels**, and they shall gather **out of his kingdom** all things that **offend**, and them which **do iniquity**. *Ref. Matthews 13:41-43*

- The **kingdom of heaven** is like unto a **net**, that was cast into the **sea**, and gathered of every kind...and gathered the **good** into vessels, but cast the **bad** away. So shall it be at the end of the world: the **angels** shall come forth, and **sever the wicked from among the just.** *Ref. Matthews 13:47-49*

- When the **Son of man** shall come in his glory, and **all the holy angels** with him ... and before him shall be **gathered all nations**: and **he shall separate them** one from another, as a **shepherd** divideth ***his* sheep** from the **goats**: and he shall set the **sheep** on his right hand, but the **goats** on the left.

  Then shall the King say unto <u>**them on his right hand**</u>, come, ye blessed of my Father, inherit the kingdom prepared for you from the foundation of the world. *Ref. Matthews 25:31-34*

- Then shall he say also unto <u>**them on the left hand**</u>, depart from me, ye cursed, into everlasting fire, prepared for the devil and his angels: For I was an **hungered,** and ye gave me no meat: I was **thirsty**, and ye gave me no drink: I was a **stranger**, and ye took me not in: **naked**, and ye clothed me not: **sick**, and **in prison**, and ye visited me not...when saw we thee...inasmuch as **you did *it* not to one of the least of these, ye did *it* not to me.** *Ref. Matthews 25:41-45*

- Two *men* shall be in the field; **the one shall be taken, and the other left**. *Ref. Luke 17:36*

CPSIA information can be obtained
at www.ICGtesting.com
Printed in the USA
BVHW060029180722
642290BV00007B/152